01

KNOCK, KNOCK.

Who's there?

Howard.

Howard who?

Howard you like to join me for a Hyrox workout? I promise it's only slightly more intense than climbing Everest.

02

HOW DO YOU SPOT A HYROXER AT A PARTY?

They're the ones pushing the couch across the room for fun.

03

WHY WAS THE HYROXER AT THE GROCERY STORE SO RELAXED?

They mistook the Farmers Carry for a shopping spree.

04

I TOLD MY FRIEND I COMPLETED A HYROX WORKOUT WITHOUT BREAKING A SWEAT.

He said, "That's impossible!" I replied, "Exactly, I never started."

05

HAVE YOU NOTICED THAT HYROXERS USE TERMS LIKE "FUN" AND "EASY" DIFFERENTLY THAN THE REST OF US?

Their "fun" includes a marathon of pain and their "easy" is our "I need a week off."

06

A HYROX WORKOUT IS THE ANSWER TO THE QUESTION

"What combines the joy of exercise with the sensation of narrowly escaping a bear?"

07

I JOINED A HYROX WORKOUT THINKING IT WAS A NEW YOGA CLASS.

The only thing that stretched was my realization of how unprepared I was.

08

ME: "I CAN TOTALLY KEEP UP WITH A HYROX WORKOUT."

Also me, after 10 minutes: "Is it too late to change my identity and move to a country where Hyrox doesn't exist?"

09

WELCOME TO HYROX, WHERE THE WEIGHTS ARE HEAVY

And the only thing heavier is the pressure to not look tired.

10

LAST TIME I DID A HYROX WORKOUT, I FOUND MUSCLES HURTING I DIDN'T EVEN KNOW EXISTED.

I'm now convinced my body is made up of 90% undiscovered muscles.

11

KNOCK, KNOCK.

Who's there?

Sled.

Sled who?

Sled me borrow some energy, I've pushed mine all the way to the finish line.

12

HOW DO HYROXERS SPICE UP THEIR LOVE LIFE?

With burpee broad jumps in the bedroom!

13

EVER NOTICE HOW HYROXERS CALL A BRUTAL WORKOUT 'REFRESHING'?

That's like calling a hurricane a 'gentle breeze'.

14

I THOUGHT DOING A SLED PUSH IN HYROX WOULD BE LIKE PUSHING A CHILD'S SLED DOWN A HILL.

Turns out it's more like pushing a car... uphill... in a snowstorm.

15

JOINED A HYROX WORKOUT TO MEET FIT PEOPLE.

Halfway through, I was too busy praying for survival to remember anyone's name.

16

HOW DO YOU MAKE A HYROXER FLINCH?

Whisper '100m Sandbag Lunges' in their ear.

17

WHY DON'T HYROXERS PLAY BASKETBALL?

Because after Wall Balls, even NBA players seem like they're taking it easy.

18

WHY ARE HYROXERS BAD AT FIRST DATES?

They start with SkiErg and leave no energy for the 'after workout'.

19

WHY DO HYROXERS EXCEL IN THE BEDROOM?

Years of practicing explosive movements with Burpee Broad Jumps.

20

HYROXERS ARE GREAT AT COMMITMENTS.

Whether it's the last If they can stick with 1000m of Rowing, they can handle anything.rep or the final moments in the bedroom.

21

WHAT'S A HYROXER'S IDEA OF A NIGHTMARE?

A dream where the sled push is uphill both ways.

22

HOW DO HYROXERS WRITE LOVE LETTERS?

"Roses are red, violets are blue, if I can pull a sled, imagine what I can do for you."

23

WHY DO HYROXERS MAKE TERRIBLE SOCCER PLAYERS?

They keep trying to push the goalpost instead of the ball.

24

HYROXERS' FAVORITE PICKUP LINE:

"Are you a sled? Because I feel like I've been pulling you all day."

25

WHY DID THE HYROXER GET KICKED OUT OF THE LONG JUMP TEAM?

They kept adding burpees to every jump!

26

YOU KNOW YOU'RE A HYROXER

When rowing 1000m is your idea of a 'quick break'.

27

WHY DO HYROXERS HATE PLAYING DODGEBALL?

Because the Wall Balls don't throw back.

28

WHY ARE HYROXERS BAD AT HIDE AND SEEK?

They just keep running until they're found.

29

"I'M INTO FITNESS," SAID THE HYROXER.

"Fitness whole SkiErg session into my lunch break."

30

YOU KNOW YOU'RE A HYROXER

When your idea of a 'light workout' is someone else's 'near-death experience'.

31

I TRIED HYROX ONCE.

I was expecting a pat on the back but got a reality check instead.

32

HYROX WORKOUTS ARE LIKE HORROR MOVIES

Just when you think it's over, there's one more scare.

33

ME: "I'LL TRY HYROX, IT'LL BE FUN," THEY SAID.

Also me, during the workout: "Define 'fun' again?"

34

WELCOME TO HYROX

Where the only thing heavier than the weights is your regret the next morning.

35

TRIED HYROX FOR THE FIRST TIME.

They know how to "pI used to have a life, now I have a foam roller.ush the pace" in more ways than one.

36

WATCHING ME DO A SKIERG IS LIKE WATCHING A PENGUIN TRY TO FLY.

Ambitious but futile.

37

"I LOVE RELAXING"

Says the Hyroxer, as they annihilate the concept of 'rest' with another round of lunges.

38

HYROX?

It's a piece of cake, if the cake was made of sweat and despair.

39

ONE HYROX SESSION IS ENOUGH WORKOUT FOR TWO LIFETIMES,

According to my now-retired muscles.

40

A HYROXER'S MOTTO:

"Why do it the easy way when you can make it a workout?"

41

IN A WORLD OBSESSED WITH EFFICIENCY

Hyroxers are the only people who find joy in prolonging physical agony.

42

KNOCK, KNOCK.

Who's there?

Water.

Water who?

Water you waiting for? Let's hit another Hyrox session!

43

JOINING HYROX IS LIKE SIGNING UP FOR A ROLLER COASTER

Except the screaming is your muscles.

44

I THOUGHT HYROX WOULD BE A WALK IN THE PARK.

Turns out, it's more like a sprint through a minefield.

45

HYROX WORKOUTS ARE THE PHYSICAL EQUIVALENT OF

"This is fine" as everything burns around you.

46

THAT MOMENT WHEN YOU REALIZE

Your Hyrox warm-up is someone else's entire workout.

47

MY FIRST HYROX WORKOUT WAS LIKE A FIRST DATE:

Nervous, sweaty, and I wasn't sure if there'd be a second.

48

ME DOING WALL BALLS IS LIKE A GLITCH IN THE MATRIX:

Nothing seems to work the way it's supposed to.

49

WHY DON'T HYROXERS LIKE COLD WEATHER?

They've had enough of the 'chill' from the SkiErg.

50

HYROXERS' FAVORITE LOVE STORY:

"Pushing a sled and falling in love with the ground after every rep."

51

WHY ARE BATHROOMS AT HYROX COMPETITIONS ALWAYS OCCUPIED?

Sled pushes make everyone want to 'push' a little more.

52

WALL BALLS IN HYROX:

Where you throw your frustrations at the wall, and the wall throws them right back.

53

AFTER A HYROX RUNNING SESSION

The real race is getting to the bathroom first.

54

WHY DON'T HYROXERS MAKE GOOD SECRET AGENTS?

They can't help but spill their 'personal bests' in every conversation.

55

A HYROXER'S DIET:

If it doesn't make you faster, stronger, or feel like you're on fire, it's not on the menu.

56

HYROXERS ARE LIKE A CULT

But the only thing they sacrifice is their free time... and maybe their knees.

57

YOU CAN SPOT A HYROXER FROM A MILE AWAY.

They're the ones where 90% of their wardrobe says 'sweat is just fat crying'.

58

HYROXERS DON'T NEED ALARM CLOCKS.

Their muscle soreness wakes them up just fine.

59

FOR HYROXERS

'Friendly competition' means 'I'll be friendly after I beat your time'.

60

HYROXERS DON'T HAVE HOBBIES.

They have Hyrox. And if they have time for anything else, they're not doing Hyrox right.

61

A HYROXER'S POST-WORKOUT ROUTINE:

Hydrate, contemplate life choices, repeat.

62

WHY DON'T HYROXERS BELIEVE IN TAKING SHORTCUTS?

Because the longer route has more opportunities for burpees.

63

HYROX IS WHERE

'I'll just do a light workout today' translates to 'I might only pass out once'.

64

A HYROXER'S IDEA OF A RECOVERY DAY

Is only doing half of their usual workout.

65

HYROXERS BELIEVE PAIN IS JUST WEAKNESS LEAVING THE BODY

Along with their ability to walk normally the next day.

66

WHY DO HYROXERS STRUGGLE WITH QUIET MEDITATION?

Because in their world, 'inner peace' is just the rest between sets.

67

WHAT DO YOU CALL A HYROXER WHO JUST WON A COMPETITION?

A 'sore' winner!

68

EVER NOTICE HOW HYROXERS USE KETTLEBELLS LIKE SOME PEOPLE USE SMARTPHONES?

Constantly and with intense focus.

69

TRIED A HYROX WORKOUT.

Now I understand why some animals play dead.

70

ME BEFORE HYROX: "I'M IN PRETTY GOOD SHAPE."

Me after Hyrox: "I've made a terrible mistake."

71

WELCOME TO HYROX

Where every day is leg day, and every night is a prayer for mercy.

72

A HYROXER WALKS INTO A BAR...

but only because it was part of the obstacle course.

73

WATCHING ME DO A FARMER'S CARRY IS LIKE WATCHING A TODDLER CARRY GROCERIES:

A lot of wobbling and eventual collapse.

74

"I JOINED HYROX FOR FUN," I SAID.

Now, my definition of 'fun' is when it's over.

75

KNOCK, KNOCK.

Who's there?
PR.
PR who?
PR-epare yourself for a new personal record!

76

IN THE WORLD OF HYROX

'Taking it easy' is just a myth, like unicorns or comfortable burpees.

77

HYROXERS ARE LIKE OVEREAGER LOVERS:

They go hard and fast, and leave you wondering what just happened.

78

"I LOVE MY HYROX WORKOUT ROUTINE,"

I say, masking the existential dread with a smile.

79

MY MUSCLES WERE SO SORE AFTER HYROX

They filed a restraining order against me.

80

IF A HYROX WORKOUT WAS A MOVIE

It'd be a cross between a comedy and a horror - but mostly a horror.

81

HYROXERS DURING A WORKOUT ARE LIKE STOCK TRADERS DURING A MARKET CRASH:

Lots of shouting, sweating, and questioning life choices.

82

WHY ARE HYROXERS BAD AT CHESS?

Because they're too used to making 'power moves' instead of strategic ones.

83

KNOCK, KNOCK.

Who's there?
Howard.
Howard who?
Howard you like to recover after that Hyrox session?

84

HYROX:

Where 'catch your breath' means you've probably lost it somewhere between the sled push and the wall balls.

85

YOU CAN ALWAYS TELL A HYROXER'S CAR:

It's the one with the foam roller in the back seat.

86

I THOUGHT HYROX WOULD IMPROVE MY SOCIAL LIFE

But my only new friends are aches and pains.

87

HYROX IS LIKE A ROLLER COASTER

Except the screams are real and the fear is for your muscles.

88

SIGNED UP FOR HYROX THINKING IT WAS A NEW HYDRATION DRINK.

I've never been more wrong in my life.

89

HYROX:

Because who needs a calm morning when you can have a heart-pounding, sweat-dripping start to your day?

90

ME DOING SKIERG

Looks like I'm trying to start an invisible lawnmower.

91

HYROX WORKOUTS ARE LIKE ABSTRACT ART:

Confusing, intense, and you're not sure if you're doing it right.

92

"I'M DOING HYROX FOR RELAXATION"

Said no one ever.

93

HYROX:

Where 'stretch your limits' isn't just a phrase, it's a painful reality.

94

WHY DO HYROXERS AVOID DATING APPS?

They're already committed to the most demanding relationship: their workout schedule.

95

"I LOVE HYROX"

I say, as I mentally prepare for the next round of existential gym dread.

96

IF HYROX WAS A BOOK

It'd be titled "A Thousand Ways to Sweat and Cry".

97

A HYROX WORKOUT IS LIKE A UNICORN

Magical, mythical, and leaves you wondering if it's really happening.

98

KNOCK, KNOCK.

Who's there?

Noah.

Noah who?

Noah good place where we can do some sled pulls?

99

HYROX:

Where "feel the burn" is not just a catchphrase, it's a daily reality.

100

YOU CAN TELL SOMEONE'S A HYROXER

When their idea of a 'light snack' is a protein shake and five minutes of planking.

Copyright © 2023 by The 100 Book Club – www.100bookclub.com

All rights reserved.

No portion of this book may be reproduced in any form without written permission from the publisher or author, except as permitted by copyright law.

Printed in Great Britain
by Amazon